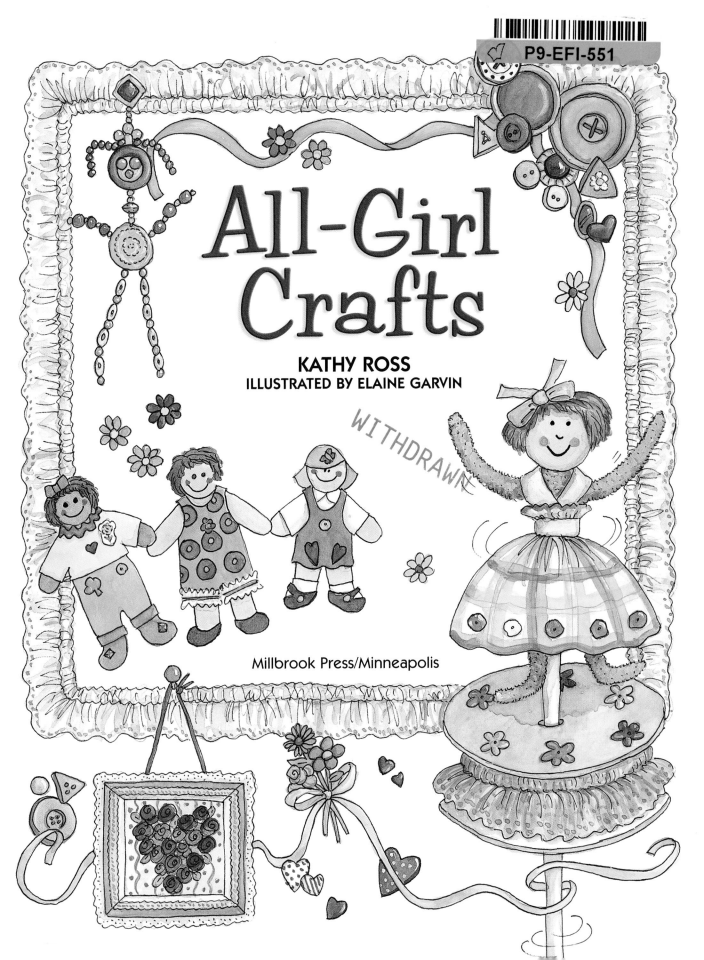

All-Girl Crafts

KATHY ROSS
ILLUSTRATED BY ELAINE GARVIN

Millbrook Press/Minneapolis

In memory of Elaine, with thanks for her beautiful work.   KR

For my three grandgirls—my granddaughter Eleanor,

and my grandnieces Danielle and McKenzie.   EG

Millbrook Press
A division of Lerner Publishing Group
241 First Avenue North
Minneapolis, MN 55401 U.S.A.

Website address: www.lernerbooks.com

Library of Congress Cataloging-in-Publication Data

Ross, Kathy (Katharine Reynolds), 1948-
  All-girl crafts / Kathy Ross ; illustrated by Elaine Garvin.
    p. cm.
Summary: Provides step-by-step directions for twenty-two crafts designed for those who are
    interested in fashion, decor, dolls, and jewelry.
ISBN–13: 978–0–7613–2776–9 (lib. bdg.)
ISBN–10: 0–7613–2776–2 (lib. bdg.)
1. Handicraft for girls—Juvenile literature. [1. Handicraft.] I.Garvin, Elaine, ill. II. Title.
TT171.R68 2006
745.5—dc22   2003011886

Manufactured in the United States of America
1 2 3 4 5 6—DP—11 10 09 08 07 06

Contents

Peek-a-Boo Envelopes

Turn ordinary envelopes into extraordinary ones with this idea.

Here is what you need:

envelopes

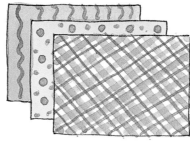
patterned wrapping paper
or scrapbook paper

scissors

white
craft glue

shape punches

1. Use a shape punch to punch shapes through both sides of the envelope on the bottom and/or side edges.

2. You can also punch a shape in the flap of the envelope.

3. Fold a piece of patterned paper in half, patterned side out. Cut the folded paper so that it fits inside the envelope to line it so that the pattern shows through the punched shapes.

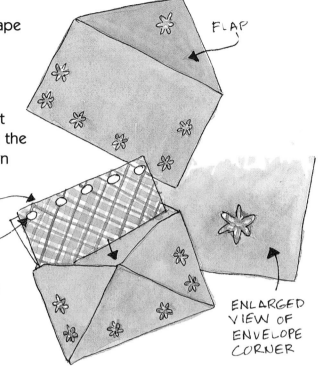

FLAP

PATTERNED LINER

DABS OF GLUE

ENLARGED VIEW OF ENVELOPE CORNER

4. Secure the liner with dabs of glue.

5. Cut a square of patterned paper to glue on the inside of the envelope flap to show through the punched shape.

Use seasonal shape punches to make special envelopes for different times of the year.

Pillow Doll Pajama Bag

**Let one of your pretty dolls help you
store your pajamas until bedtime.**

Here is what you need:

old round pillow

scissors

white craft glue

GLUE

lace, ribbon, and trims

sticky-back Velcro strip

doll that is shorter than the width of the pillow

small fake flowers

Here is what you do:

1. Cut a slit across the center of the back of the pillow. Remove all the stuffing and save it to use with another craft project.

PILLOW BACK

SLIT

STUFFING

2. Attach a strip of the Velcro to each side of the cut so that the pillow can be closed when the two sides of the Velcro are stuck together.

SHORT SLIT

PILLOW FRONT

3. Cut a slit across the center of the front side of the pillow that is just large enough to slip the doll into up to the waist. The round pillow should look like the full skirt of the doll.

4. Glue lace, ribbon, and other trims around the edge of the pillow to decorate the "skirt." If the pillow you are using already has a ruffle around the edge, you can decorate that, too.

5. Tie a ribbon bow around the fake flowers and glue them to the bottom of one side of the skirt.

SLIP DOLL INTO PILLOW

PILLOW BOTTOM

6. Slip the doll into the front of the pillow. Tuck your pajamas inside the pillow to store them out of sight until bedtime. Stand the pillow doll up in front of the pillows on your bed.

You can decorate the skirt with jewels, buttons, or felt shapes. Decorate your pillow doll to reflect your own imaginative style.

7

Tassel Doll

Try hanging a tassel doll from a dresser knob, curtain hook, or light chain—even off your diary key!

Here is what you need:

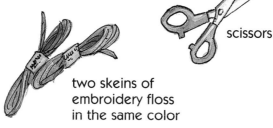

scissors

wooden bead with large hole

two skeins of embroidery floss in the same color

embroidery floss for hair

markers

tiny fake flowers

Here is what you do:

1. Cut a 1-foot-long (30-cm) piece of floss from the end of one skein. Slide the piece of floss between the two sides of the folded skein of floss at one end of the skein and tie it in a knot. Tie the two ends together to become the hanger for the doll.

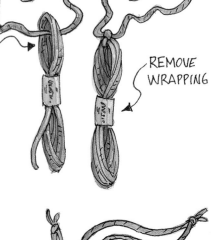

REMOVE WRAPPING

2. Thread the hanger through the bead. Pull the bead down over the top of the fold of the skein of floss, to become the head.

3. Use the markers to draw a face on the bead head.

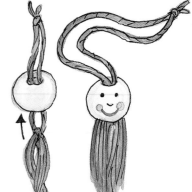

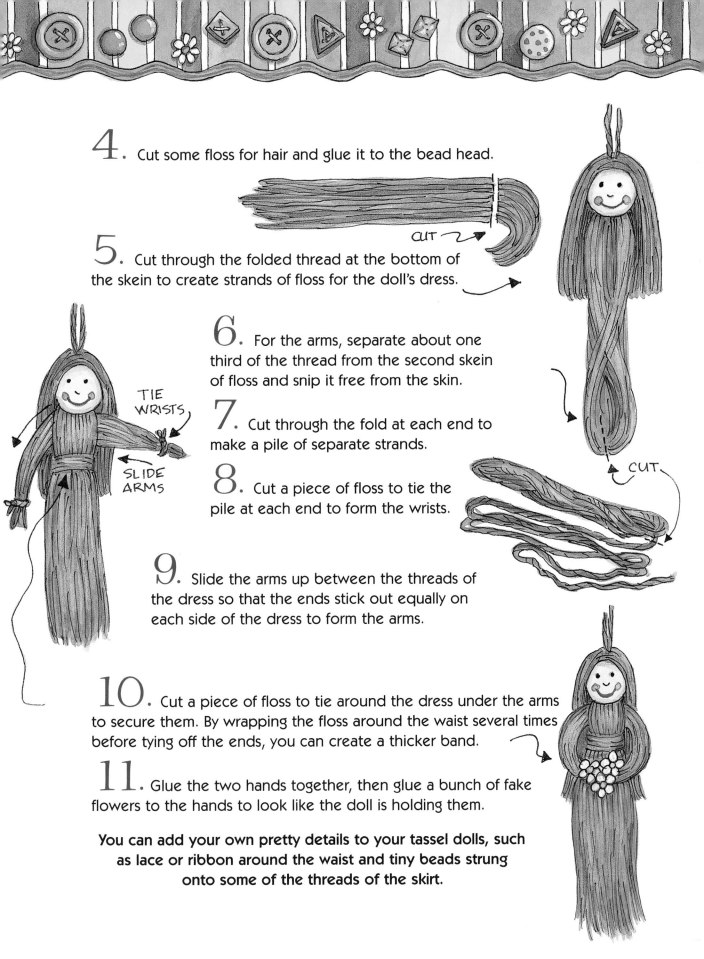

4. Cut some floss for hair and glue it to the bead head.

CUT

5. Cut through the folded thread at the bottom of the skein to create strands of floss for the doll's dress.

6. For the arms, separate about one third of the thread from the second skein of floss and snip it free from the skin.

7. Cut through the fold at each end to make a pile of separate strands.

TIE WRISTS

8. Cut a piece of floss to tie the pile at each end to form the wrists.

SLIDE ARMS

CUT

9. Slide the arms up between the threads of the dress so that the ends stick out equally on each side of the dress to form the arms.

10. Cut a piece of floss to tie around the dress under the arms to secure them. By wrapping the floss around the waist several times before tying off the ends, you can create a thicker band.

11. Glue the two hands together, then glue a bunch of fake flowers to the hands to look like the doll is holding them.

You can add your own pretty details to your tassel dolls, such as lace or ribbon around the waist and tiny beads strung onto some of the threads of the skirt.

Flower Fairies

Make a few fairies to fly around your room.

Here is what you need:

fabric flowers

scissors

sharp permanent markers

¾-inch (2-cm) wooden beads

white craft glue

thin craft ribbons

Here is what you do:

1. Choose one flower to become the skirt for the flower fairy. Trim the stem so that it is about 2 inches (5 cm) long.

CUT

SLIDE PETALS UP & OFF THE STEM

2. Take apart two or three different flowers by pulling out the plastic centers and pulling the layers of petals from the flower stem.

3. Turn the flower dress so that the stem is at the top. Layer three or four different-sized petals, starting with the largest petal, and sliding them over the stem of the flower.

4. Use the markers to draw a face on one side of the wooden bead for the head. Slide the head onto the stem of the flower and secure it with some glue.

SMALL PETAL CIRCLE

GLUE

5. Slide a small circle of flower petals onto the stem to become a hat for the flower fairy. Secure the hat with a dab of glue.

6. Cut two identical leaves from a flower. Glue the end of each leaf to the back of the flower dress, just below the head, so that they stick out to form the wings for the fairy.

7. Tie a length of thin ribbon in a bow around the neck of the fairy.

BACK OF FAIRY

8. Make a hanger for the flower fairy by tying one end of an 18-inch (46-cm) length of ribbon to the stem.

A flower fairy makes a beautiful package tie for an extra special friend.

Doll Furniture Makeover

Turn dull dollhouse furniture into works of art!

Here is what you need:

wooden doll furniture

acrylic craft paint and fine paintbrushes

Styrofoam tray to work on

felt and fabric scraps

scissors

white craft glue

tiny stickers

trims and ribbon

Here is what you do:

1. Use one or more colors to paint a piece of doll furniture either a different color or with a design of colors.

2. Use the felt and fabric scraps to cover chair seats and tops of tables.

3. Use the tiny stickers as furniture decals.

4. Use the trims to decorate the edges of the furniture.

Check your collage box to see what other things you might use to give tired old doll furniture a face-lift.

Dancing Doll Puppet

If you use a lot of craft ribbon you will be happy to discover this creative way to use the empty ribbon spools.

Here is what you need:

two 12-inch (30-cm) pipe cleaners

scissors

permanent markers

white craft glue

¾-inch (2-cm) wooden bead

plastic straw

embroidery floss for hair

thin craft ribbon

colored or patterned tissue paper

sequins

empty cardboard ribbon spool

construction paper scrap

ruffle lace trim

Here is what you do:

7 INCHES   **3 INCHES**

1. Cut a 7-inch (18-cm) piece of pipe cleaner for the body and legs of the dancing doll. Fold the piece in half and fold out the two ends to form the feet.

2. Cut a 3-inch (8-cm) piece of pipe cleaner. Wrap the center of the piece of pipe cleaner around the top part of the legs so that the ends stick out on each side to form the arms.

3. Use the permanent markers to draw a face on one side of the wooden bead. Glue the bead to the top of the folded leg piece for the head.

INSERT

12 INCH PIPE CLEANER

4. Slide one end of a 12-inch (30-cm) pipe cleaner into the hole in the head bead and secure it with glue.

5. Cut bits of embroidery floss. Glue the bits to the head of the doll for hair.

6. Make a tiny bow from the craft ribbon to glue in the hair on one side.

7. Cut a 2-inch (5-cm) piece of ribbon and wrap it around the neck of the doll so that the two ends come down in front to form the top of a dress.

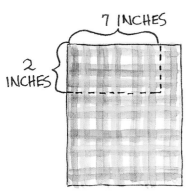

7 INCHES

2 INCHES

8.
Cut a 2- by 7-inch (5- by 18-cm) strip of tissue paper for a skirt for the doll. Gather one long side together around the waist of the doll to make a full skirt. Secure the skirt to the doll with dabs of glue. Tie a ribbon in a bow around the waist of the doll.

BACK

TRACED & CUT OUT CONSTRUCTION PAPER

GLUE

9.
Trace around one side of the ribbon spool on the construction paper. Cut out the circle. Glue the paper to the spool to cover one side.

10.
Glue the ruffle lace around the center core of the spool to cover it.

11.
Glue sequins to the skirt of the doll and the top of the covered ribbon spool to decorate.

SLIDE STRAW UP

12.
Slide the long pipe cleaner coming down from the bottom of the doll through the plastic straw. Trim off any excess pipe cleaner.

13.
Poke the straw through the paper covering the hole in the center of the spool, so that the straw end hangs down through the spool and the feet of the doll rest on top of the spool.

To make the little doll dance, hold the spool in one hand and twist, push, and pull on the end of the straw so that the doll moves up and down and twirls around.

Delightfully Decorated Doll Stand

Give doll stands a different look for each season of the year.

Here is what you need:

ballpoint pen

scissors

thin craft ribbon and other trims

doll stand

white craft glue

felt in different colors

sticky-back Velcro

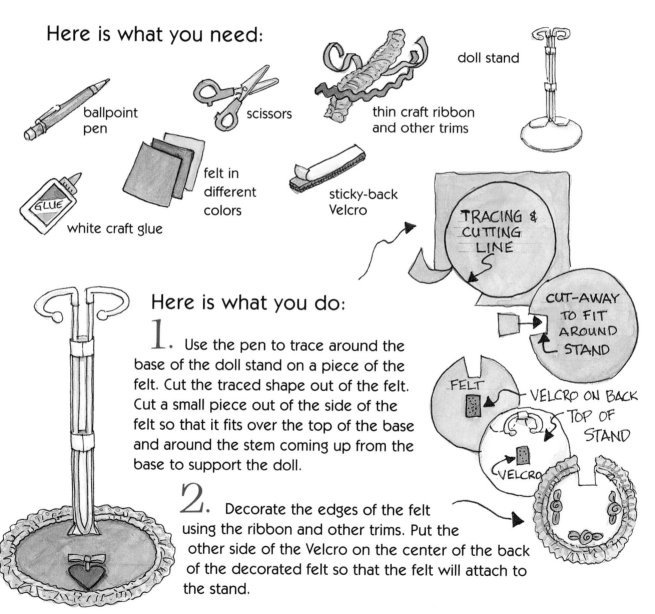

TRACING & CUTTING LINE

CUT-AWAY TO FIT AROUND STAND

FELT

VELCRO ON BACK TOP OF STAND

VELCRO

Here is what you do:

1. Use the pen to trace around the base of the doll stand on a piece of the felt. Cut the traced shape out of the felt. Cut a small piece out of the side of the felt so that it fits over the top of the base and around the stem coming up from the base to support the doll.

2. Decorate the edges of the felt using the ribbon and other trims. Put the other side of the Velcro on the center of the back of the decorated felt so that the felt will attach to the stand.

Make lots of different felt covers for the doll stand and change the cover when you change your doll's outfit.

Seashell Baby

Turn last summer's beach bounty into a sweet little baby, complete with ruffled bonnet.

Here is what you need:

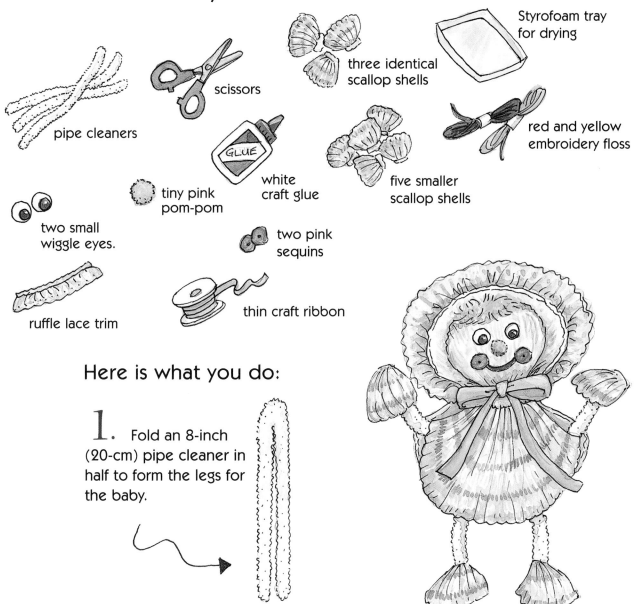

three identical scallop shells

Styrofoam tray for drying

scissors

pipe cleaners

GLUE

white craft glue

five smaller scallop shells

red and yellow embroidery floss

tiny pink pom-pom

two small wiggle eyes.

two pink sequins

ruffle lace trim

thin craft ribbon

Here is what you do:

1. Fold an 8-inch (20-cm) pipe cleaner in half to form the legs for the baby.

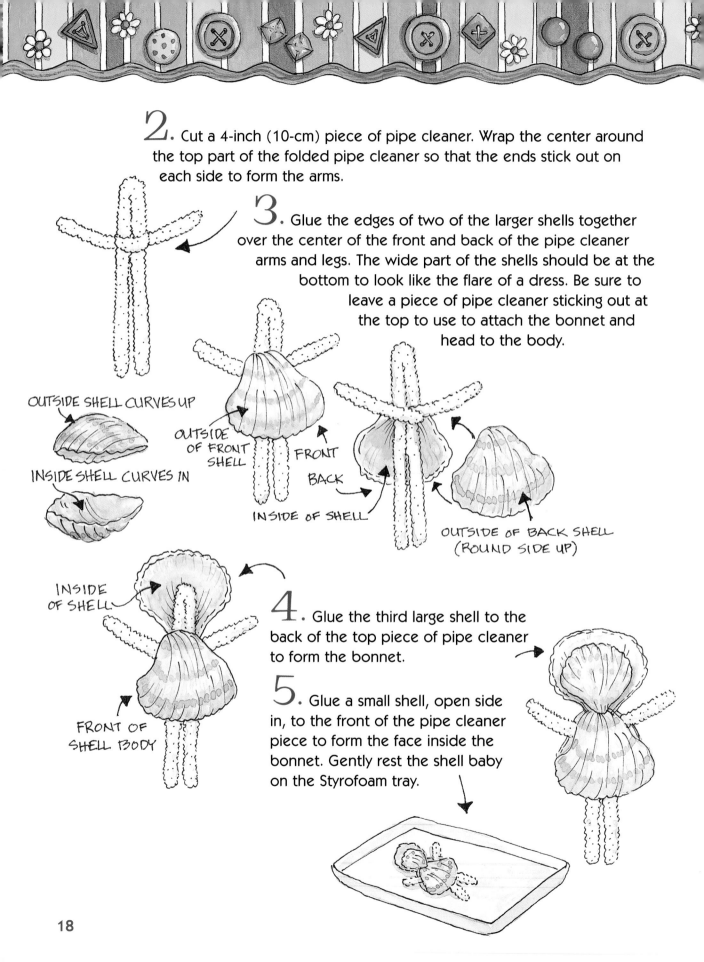

2. Cut a 4-inch (10-cm) piece of pipe cleaner. Wrap the center around the top part of the folded pipe cleaner so that the ends stick out on each side to form the arms.

3. Glue the edges of two of the larger shells together over the center of the front and back of the pipe cleaner arms and legs. The wide part of the shells should be at the bottom to look like the flare of a dress. Be sure to leave a piece of pipe cleaner sticking out at the top to use to attach the bonnet and head to the body.

OUTSIDE SHELL CURVES UP

INSIDE SHELL CURVES IN

OUTSIDE OF FRONT SHELL

FRONT

BACK

INSIDE OF SHELL

OUTSIDE OF BACK SHELL (ROUND SIDE UP)

INSIDE OF SHELL

FRONT OF SHELL BODY

4. Glue the third large shell to the back of the top piece of pipe cleaner to form the bonnet.

5. Glue a small shell, open side in, to the front of the pipe cleaner piece to form the face inside the bonnet. Gently rest the shell baby on the Styrofoam tray.

GLOB OF GLUE

INSIDE OF SHELL

OUTSIDE OF SHELL

6. Glue the back of the end of each arm to the inside of a small shell to make the hands.

7. Glue the other two small shells, open side down, on the end of each leg. Let the glue dry completely before bending the shells forward to form the feet.

8. Cut some bits of yellow floss for the hair for the baby. Glue the hair to the top of the head.

GLUE TO SHELL BACK

BACK VIEW

9. Glue the two wiggle eyes to the face. Glue the tiny pom-pom below the eyes for a nose.

10. Glue a tiny piece of red thread for the mouth. Glue the thread to the face in the shape of a smile. Glue a sequin cheek to each side of the smile.

11. Glue a piece of the ruffle lace around the edge of the shell bonnet.

12. Tie a piece of the thin ribbon in a bow. Glue the bow at the neck of the shell baby to look like the ties for the bonnet.

Now that you know how to make the shell baby, try making some other members of the shell people family.

Sensational Storage Box

Turn an ordinary shoe box into an extraordinary one with this idea.

Here is what you need:

- clear plastic blister pack from battery package or other product
- pencil
- shoe box with a lid
- scissors
- craft paint and a paintbrush
- newspaper to work on
- felt
- masking tape
- artificial flowers
- pretty ribbons and trims
- construction paper
- white craft glue

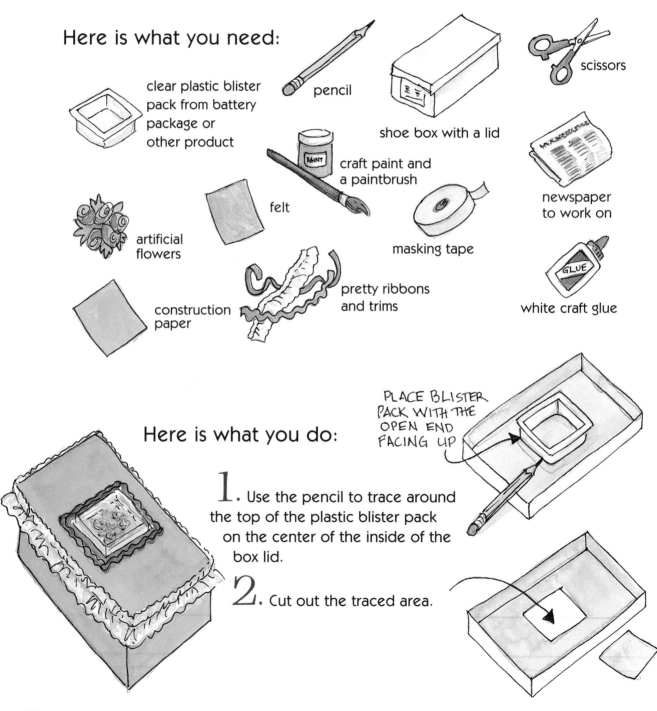

Here is what you do:

PLACE BLISTER PACK WITH THE OPEN END FACING UP

1. Use the pencil to trace around the top of the plastic blister pack on the center of the inside of the box lid.

2. Cut out the traced area.

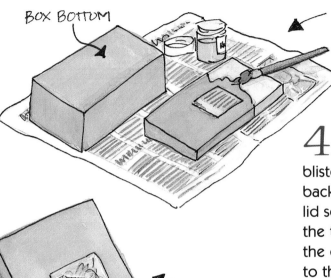

BOX BOTTOM

3. Paint the outside of the shoe box and the lid. Allow the paint to dry before continuing.

4. Push the top of the blister pack through the back of the opening in the lid so that it sticks out from the top of the lid. Secure the edges of the blister pack to the inside of the lid using masking tape.

5. Arrange the flowers in the blister pack so that they look pretty when viewed through the plastic from the top of the lid.

6. Cover the opening in the back of the lid with construction paper glued around the edges. Line the entire inside of the lid by gluing on construction paper or felt.

CONSTRUCTION PAPER COVER

FELT LINING

7. Decorate the edges of the lid and around the blister pack using various trims and ribbons. You can also glue trims around the box if you wish.

These boxes make wonderful storage containers for doll clothes, letters, craft supplies, and a zillion other things you will probably think of. Better make several of them!

Jewelry Doll Jar

Collect a stash of old costume jewelry to make this next project.

Here is what you need:

white craft glue

scissors

large jar

collection
of junk jewelry

Here is what you do:

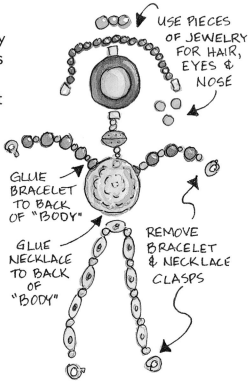

1. Arrange different pieces of jewelry into a jewelry doll. Large round earrings are perfect for the face. Bend the clasp back and forth to remove it from the back of the earring.

USE PIECES OF JEWELRY FOR HAIR, EYES & NOSE

2. Glue on individual beads cut from a necklace to make a face.

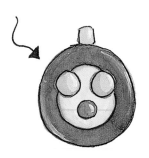

GLUE BRACELET TO BACK OF "BODY"

GLUE NECKLACE TO BACK OF "BODY"

REMOVE BRACELET & NECKLACE CLASPS

HAIR →

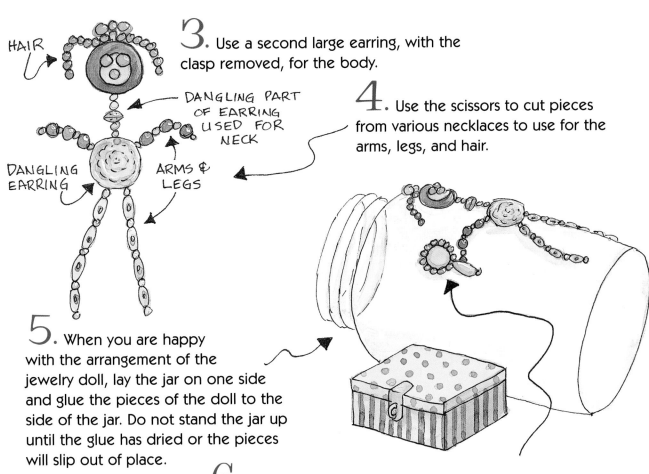

3. Use a second large earring, with the clasp removed, for the body.

DANGLING PART OF EARRING USED FOR NECK

DANGLING EARRING

ARMS & LEGS

4. Use the scissors to cut pieces from various necklaces to use for the arms, legs, and hair.

5. When you are happy with the arrangement of the jewelry doll, lay the jar on one side and glue the pieces of the doll to the side of the jar. Do not stand the jar up until the glue has dried or the pieces will slip out of place.

HINT: PLACE A FLAT OBJECT LIKE A JEWELRY BOX OR BOOK ON EACH SIDE OF THE JAR TO KEEP IT FROM ROLLING

6. Bend the stem of a flower-shaped pierced earring to the side. Glue the earring to the end of one arm to look like a flower.

7. Decorate the rest of the jar with backless earrings and other pieces of jewelry.

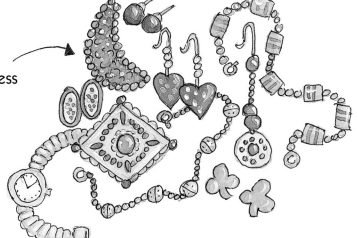

Keep the decorated jar on your dresser to catch all those odds and ends that seem to accumulate so quickly.

Bangles Picture Frame

Turn old bangle bracelets into picture-perfect photo frames.

Here is what you need:

poster board

pencil

white craft glue

three old bangle bracelets that are the same size

scissors

small artificial flowers

large seed beads

pipe cleaner or wire

Here is what you do:

1. Choose three bangle bracelets that are of identical size. Bangle bracelets are often sold in sets of three or more of the same style, so they should not be hard to find.

2. Use the pencil to trace around the outside of one of the bracelets on the poster board twice.

3. Cut out both tracings.

TRACING LINES

4. Hold one bangle on top of one of the poster board circles and trim it so that it does not show around the outside edges of the bracelet.

TRIM EDGE

TRIM AWAY AT TOP OF CARDBOARD

5. Cut away a small portion from the edge of the poster board so that there will be a thin space to slip the wire or pipe cleaner through to hold the frame together.

6. Trim the second circle to match the first one.

FIRST CIRCLE

SECOND CIRCLE

TOP BRACELET (FRAME FRONT)

GLUE

TOP OF FRAME

LEAVE SIDE SPACE OPEN

7. Glue one of the bracelets to one of the poster board circles, leaving one side of the bracelet without glue so that you will be able to slip a photo into the frame from the side.

BOTTOM BRACELET (FRAME BACK)

8. Remember that the cutaway edge of the poster board will be the top of the frame.

9. Glue a second bracelet to the back of the poster board circle. Let the glue dry.

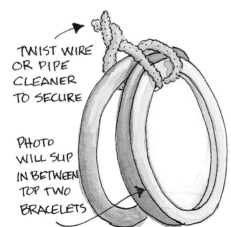

TWIST WIRE OR PIPE CLEANER TO SECURE

PHOTO WILL SLIP IN BETWEEN TOP TWO BRACELETS

10. Use two pieces of wire or pipe cleaner to attach the last bracelet to the back of the frame to use as a stand. Make sure that the wire or pipe cleaners are loose enough to allow the back bracelet to swing out from the frame to use as a stand.

...CONTINUED...

11. You can string some seed beads on the wire at the top of the frame for decoration and to conceal it. You also can cover the wire or the pipe cleaners by tucking some small artificial flowers in at the top of the frame.

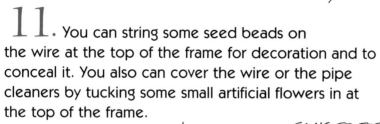

GLUE TO TOP OF FRAME

CARDBOARD

SLIP PHOTO IN THROUGH SIDE

12. Use the second piece of poster board as a pattern to cut a photo to fit in the frame. Slide the photo in through the opening that you left in the side of the frame.

YOU CAN ALSO USE OTHER DECORATING DESIGNS WITH THINGS LIKE BOWS & BEADS, PAINTED POLKA DOTS OR PAINTED FLOWERS ON THE TOP BRACELET

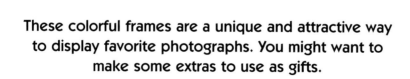

These colorful frames are a unique and attractive way to display favorite photographs. You might want to make some extras to use as gifts.

Bean Friend Change Purse

Use an old bean-filled toy to make a change purse.

Here is what you need:

small
bean-filled toy

scissors

strip of
sticky-back
Velcro

thin
craft ribbon

Here is what you do:

VIEW FROM ABOVE

VELCRO STRIPS

REMOVE BEANS

1. Cut a slit in the back of the toy. Empty out the contents. Sometimes the head has separate stuffing. In this case, you might want to leave the stuffing in the head to give the head more support.

2. Cut a strip of sticky-back Velcro as long as the cut in the toy.

3. Stick a piece of the Velcro on each side of the cut so that the opening is closed when the two sides of the Velcro are joined together.

FOLD RIBBON IN HALF & THREAD END THROUGH LOOP

4. Make the toy a necklace by cutting a 2-foot (60-cm) length of ribbon, tying it around the neck of the toy and tying the two ends together.

Open the Velcro strip to stash change and small items inside the toy, then seal the Velcro to keep the treasures safe. What a great gift to make for a child!

Dressy Note Cards

Turn old paper doll dresses into glamorous, one-of-a-kind note cards.

Here is what you need:

old paper doll dresses

scissors

GLUE

white craft glue

trims, ribbons, small jewels, lace and other collage materials

package of blank note cards and envelopes

Here is what you do:

1. Choose a paper doll dress that will fit on the front of the note card. Trim the tabs off the dress.

TABS

TRIM TABS OFF

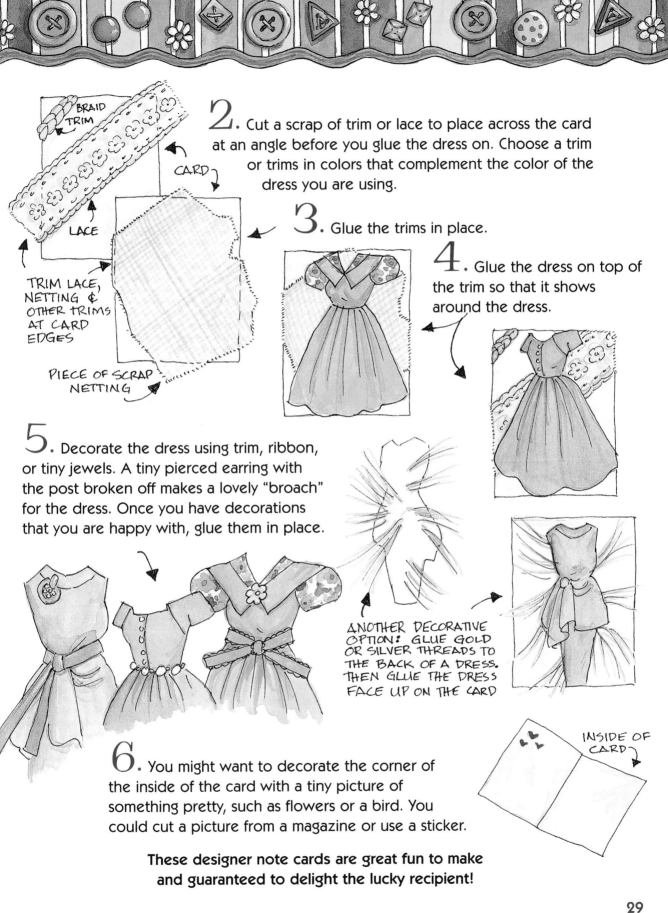

2. Cut a scrap of trim or lace to place across the card at an angle before you glue the dress on. Choose a trim or trims in colors that complement the color of the dress you are using.

3. Glue the trims in place.

4. Glue the dress on top of the trim so that it shows around the dress.

BRAID TRIM

CARD

LACE

TRIM LACE, NETTING & OTHER TRIMS AT CARD EDGES

PIECE OF SCRAP NETTING

5. Decorate the dress using trim, ribbon, or tiny jewels. A tiny pierced earring with the post broken off makes a lovely "broach" for the dress. Once you have decorations that you are happy with, glue them in place.

ANOTHER DECORATIVE OPTION: GLUE GOLD OR SILVER THREADS TO THE BACK OF A DRESS. THEN GLUE THE DRESS FACE UP ON THE CARD

6. You might want to decorate the corner of the inside of the card with a tiny picture of something pretty, such as flowers or a bird. You could cut a picture from a magazine or use a sticker.

INSIDE OF CARD

These designer note cards are great fun to make and guaranteed to delight the lucky recipient!

Scrunchy-Covered Jars

Do you have a drawerful of scrunchies? Try this crafty idea!

Here is what you need:

scissors

white craft glue

2-inch (5-cm)- and 3-inch (8-cm)-wide jars

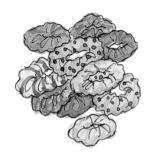

lots of colorful scrunchies

trims

artificial flowers

Here is what you do:

1. Choose five or more scrunchies of the same size and complementing colors and designs. The small ponytail scrunchies will fit over a 2-inch-wide jar, and the larger ones will fit over a 3-inch-wide jar.

2. Slide the scrunchies over the jar to cover it. Use as many scrunchies as needed for the height of the jar you are using.

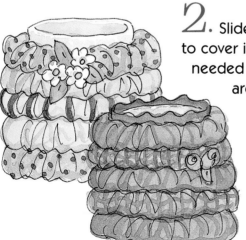

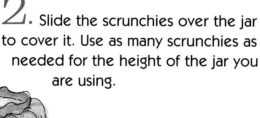

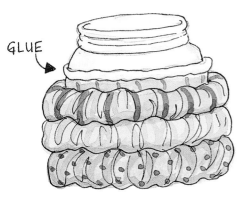

GLUE

3. You can glue the scrunchies to the jar to make a permanently decorated item. If you want to still wear the scrunchies, just slip them over the jar without glue. When you want a particular scrunchy you can slip it off the jar and replace it with another one.

TRIM ON INSIDE   GLUE ON INSIDE

4. Cut a piece of trim to glue around the rim of the jar. You can glue it around either the inside or the outside of the rim.

TRIM ON OUTSIDE

5. Tuck a small cluster of artificial flowers under the scrunchy at the top of the jar.

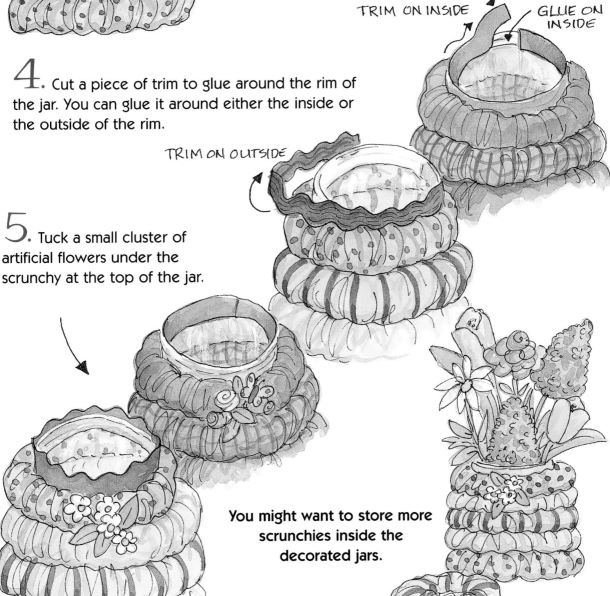

You might want to store more scrunchies inside the decorated jars.

Ribbon and Lace Doll

This is an updated version of an old-fashioned pastime.

Here is what you need:

woman paper doll from an old paper doll set, or cut from a magazine, or printed off the Internet

lots of trims, ribbon, and ruffled lace

scissors

white craft glue

masking tape

net, tiny flowers, jewels, and other pretty collage items

construction paper in three colors

light cardboard

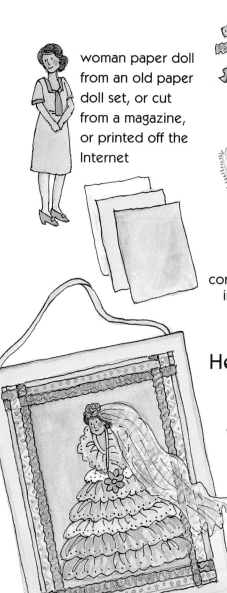

Here is what you do:

1. Wrap a piece of trim around the top of the paper doll to form the top of the gown. Glue the top in place.

2. Glue the doll to the center of a 9- by 12-inch (23- by 30-cm) sheet of construction paper.

GLUE RUFFLED LACE TO DOLL. THEN GLUE DOLL ONTO PAPER

DRAW SKIRT &
CUT OUT ALONG
DRAWN LINE

LIFT TOP LACE
& PLACE SKIRT
UNDER IT

GLUE ON
BACK OF
LACE
HEM

3. Cut a full skirt for the doll from construction paper.

4. Glue the skirt on the doll.

5. Cover the entire skirt with layers of ruffled lace.

YOU CAN DRAW GUIDE LINE
ON SKIRT FOR WHERE YOU WANT
TO GLUE DOWN THE LACE

6. Add collage items to the picture to finish dressing the doll. You might want to add flowers to her hands and a hat to her head. You can use the netting to make a long veil.

7. Glue rows of trim around the edge of the picture.

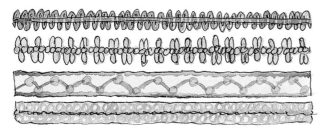

ABOVE ARE SAMPLES OF POSSIBLE PRETTY
TRIMS...RIBBONS & DECORATIVE
BRAIDS THAT YOU CAN USE.

8. Wrap a 13- by 11-inch (33- by 28-cm) piece of cardboard with a different color construction paper. Use masking tape to secure the edges at the back of the cardboard.

9. Cut a 2-foot (60-cm) length of ribbon.

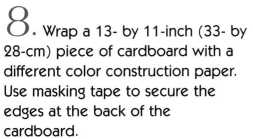

FOLD OVER TOP & BOTTOM FIRST

TOP

13 INCHES HIGH

CARDBOARD

CONSTRUCTION PAPER

BOTTOM

11 INCHES WIDE

GLUE HERE

10. Glue one end of the ribbon to the top back of each side of the covered cardboard to make a hanger.

11. Glue the smaller paper with the doll on it in the center of the covered cardboard.

Try using printed wrapping paper as one of the background papers for a pretty variation of this project.

Elegant Bookmark

Use old neckties to make beautiful fabric bookmarks.

Here is what you need:

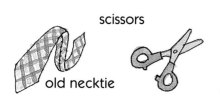

scissors

old necktie

light cardboard

white craft glue

GLUE

trim to complement pattern of necktie

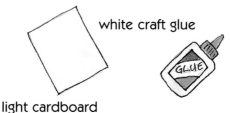

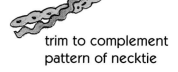

Here is what you do:

1. Cut the tip off the necktie 2 inches (5 cm) from the point.

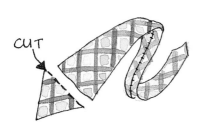

CUT

2. Cut a cardboard triangle slightly smaller than the fabric triangle cut from the necktie.

3. Slip the cardboard triangle in between the fabric and the lining of the fabric triangle. Glue the cardboard to the back of the inside lining of the fabric triangle.

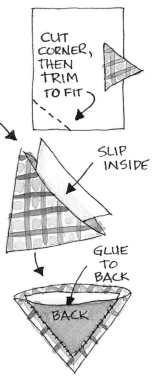

CUT CORNER, THEN TRIM TO FIT

SLIP INSIDE

GLUE TO BACK

BACK

4. Cut and glue a piece of trim along the cut edge of the front of the fabric triangle.

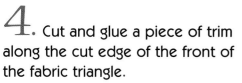

THE QUEEN OF HARTS HAS LOST SOME PARTS

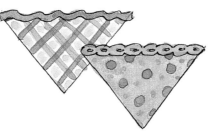

To mark a book, slip the fabric triangle over the corner of the page you want to find.

Shadow Boxes With Heart

Make two or more of these shadow boxes using different collage materials for each heart.

Here is what you need:

two or more square jewelry box bottoms; the 3½-inch (9-cm) square ones work particularly well

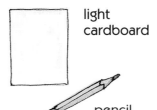
light cardboard

collage materials for each heart in shades of red, pink, or purple, such as buttons, small artificial flowers, potpourri, pom-poms, jewels, or sequins

pencil

scissors

Styrofoam tray to work on

white craft glue

ribbon, ruffle lace, and other trims

pretty printed papers

Here is what you do:

1. Use the pencil to sketch the outline of a heart on the light cardboard that is just small enough to fit in the bottom of the box.

2. Draw and cut out a heart for each shadow box you are making.

HINT: TRACE THE BOX FIRST, THEN DRAW HEART INSIDE SQUARE

HINT: DRAW A LINE DOWN MIDDLE OF BOX BEFORE DRAWING HEART

3. Cover each heart with a different collage material. When using flat items such as buttons or sequins, try to layer them to give the heart a more three-dimensional look.

4. Let the hearts dry completely on the Styrofoam tray before attempting to pick them up.

5. Cover the bottom of one or more of the boxes by gluing on a square of printed paper.

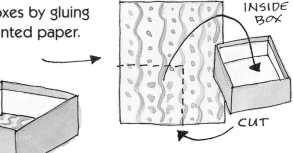

GLUE INSIDE BOX

CUT

6. Poke two small holes through each side of the bottom edge of one side of each box.

HOLES

7. Cut a 1-foot-long (30-cm) length of thin ribbon or trim for a hanger for each box. Thread the two ends of the ribbon through the two holes, starting at the inside of the box.

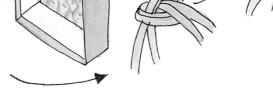

8. Tie the two ends together to make a hanger for the box.

9. Glue pretty trims around the outside and the inside edges of each box to decorate it.

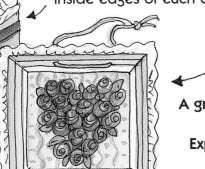

10. Glue a collage heart inside each box.

A group of these heart collage boxes look wonderful hanging on the wall. Experiment with how you might arrange them before you hang them up.

Earring Doll

Here is a great way to use old and mismatched pierced earrings.

Here is what you need:

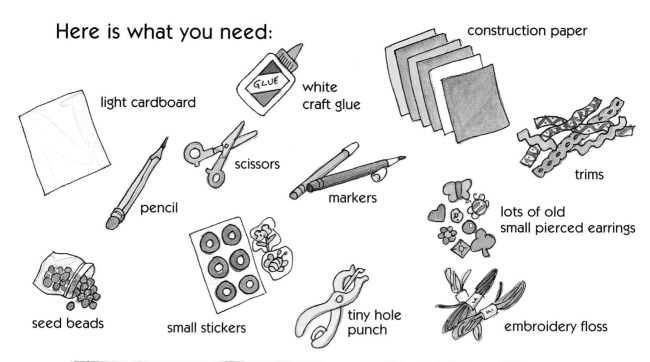

light cardboard

white craft glue

construction paper

scissors

pencil

markers

trims

lots of old small pierced earrings

seed beads

small stickers

tiny hole punch

embroidery floss

Here is what you do:

1. Use the pencil to sketch a simple doll shape on the light cardboard.

2. Cut out the shape to use as a pattern for making one or more dolls.

3. Use the pencil to trace the doll pattern on construction paper.

4. Cut out the construction paper doll.

5. If the doll seems flimsy, you may want to glue it to light cardboard to make it stiffer. When the glue dries, remove the excess cardboard around the edges of the doll.

CARDBOARD

DOLL PATTERN

CUT OUT DOLL

SKIN COLORED CONSTRUCTION PAPER

6. Use any combination of markers and collage materials to give the doll a face and hair. Embroidery floss or yarn is a good choice for hair. Small beads and sequins can be used to create a face.

7. Use the cardboard doll pattern to make clothing patterns for the doll. Use the pencil to trace around the part of the doll you want to make clothing for, then add the missing lines to complete it. For example, to make pants, trace around the outside and the inside of both legs. To finish the pants pattern, draw the line across the top for the waist of the pants and draw a line across the bottom of each leg for the cuffs of the pants.

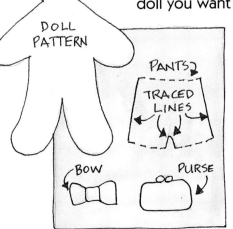

DOLL PATTERN

PANTS

TRACED LINES

BOW

PURSE

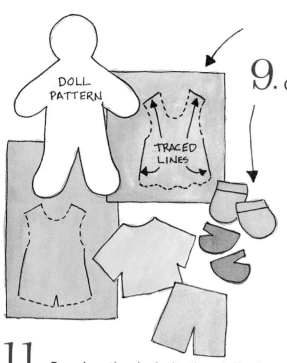

8. Trace the clothing patterns onto construction paper.

9. Cut out the clothing.

10. Use the markers, construction paper, tiny stickers, trims, and other collage materials to decorate the clothes.

11. Punch a tiny hole in the doll wherever you are going to attach clothing. You will need a hole in the top and lower center of the doll to attach dresses, shirts, and pants, in both feet for shoes and socks, and in the head for hats. You might also want to punch holes in each hand for mittens and for holding items such as a purse.

12. To punch the holes correctly in the clothing, hold the item of clothing on the doll in the position you want to attach it. Turn the doll over and use the pencil to mark the spot on the clothing where there is a hole in the doll. Punch a hole where you have marked the clothes item.

13. Use old pierced earrings to attach the clothes to the doll through the holes. The earrings add a decorative touch to the doll outfits.

14. Display your dressed doll by pressing the backs of the earrings into your bulletin board.

You can shorten this project by buying a packaged doll and clothes from the scrapbook section of your favorite craft store.

Desktop Bulletin Board

Keep saving those odd pierced earrings!

Here is what you need:

old 8- by 10-inch frame with backing and no glass

thin ribbon and trims

three 8- by 10-inch (20- by 25-cm) sheets of craft foam

scissors

white craft glue

odd stud pierced earrings

Here is what you do:

1. Stack the three sheets of craft foam, putting the color you want for the bulletin board on top.

FLIP OVER & PLACE IN FRAME

2. Remove the back of the frame and secure the stack of foam sheets in the frame with the top sheet showing through the front opening of the frame.

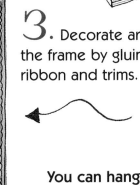

3. Decorate around the edges of the frame by gluing on strips of ribbon and trims.

4. Use old stud pierced earrings for the tacks for the bulletin board.

You can hang the bulletin board on the wall or stand it on your dresser or desk.

Button Buddy Necklace

Craft a new friend with some buttons.

Here is what you need:

colored
rubber bands

Four small, one medium, and one slightly larger colorful, flat buttons

three colors of thin craft ribbon

two tiny wiggle eyes

tiny pom-poms

scissors

white craft glue

Styrofoam tray to work on

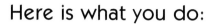

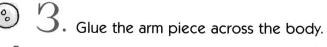

Here is what you do:

1. Cut a 4-inch (10-cm) piece of rubber band for the legs. Cut one 3-inch (8-cm) piece of rubber band for the arms and another for the body.

CUT FOR LEGS

CUT FOR ARMS & BODY

2. Fold the top of the body rubber band back to form a loop. Secure the fold by gluing the body rubber band to the Styrofoam tray.

3. Glue the arm piece across the body.

4. Fold the leg piece of rubber band into an arch and glue it to the Styrofoam tray on the end of the body piece.

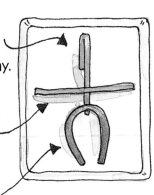

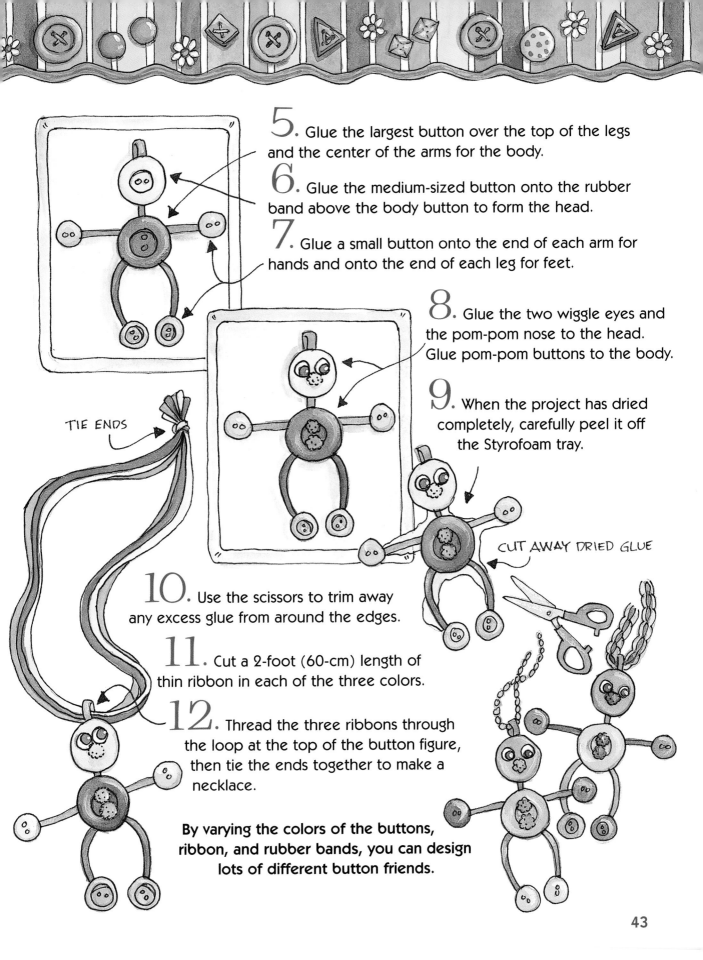

5. Glue the largest button over the top of the legs and the center of the arms for the body.

6. Glue the medium-sized button onto the rubber band above the body button to form the head.

7. Glue a small button onto the end of each arm for hands and onto the end of each leg for feet.

8. Glue the two wiggle eyes and the pom-pom nose to the head. Glue pom-pom buttons to the body.

9. When the project has dried completely, carefully peel it off the Styrofoam tray.

TIE ENDS

CUT AWAY DRIED GLUE

10. Use the scissors to trim away any excess glue from around the edges.

11. Cut a 2-foot (60-cm) length of thin ribbon in each of the three colors.

12. Thread the three ribbons through the loop at the top of the button figure, then tie the ends together to make a necklace.

By varying the colors of the buttons, ribbon, and rubber bands, you can design lots of different button friends.

High Fashion Notepad

**Paper clothing from old paper doll sets
makes charming notepads.**

Here is what you need:

stapler and staples

light cardboard

scissors

white copier paper

white craft glue

GLUE

pencil

small jewels

pipe cleaner

ribbons and trims

old paper doll dress

Here is what you do:

TRIM OFF ALL TABS

1. Trim any tabs off the dress.

2. Trace the outline of the dress on light cardboard.

3. Cut out the outline.

4. Using the cardboard dress shape as a pattern, trace the shape of the dress on the white copy paper. Stack four or five sheets of paper and cut out the shape to make the pages for your notepad. Repeat so that you will have eight or ten pages total.

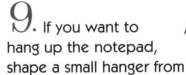

5. Staple the pages together in the center of the top portion of the dress.

6. Glue the top part of the back of the dress to the cardboard so that it forms a backing for the notepad.

7. Glue the top part of the back of the paper dress to the front of the notepad so that only the skirt will lift open.

8. Decorate the paper dress by gluing on trims, ribbon, and small jewels.

9. If you want to hang up the notepad, shape a small hanger from the pipe cleaner. Glue the hanger to the back of the top of the notepad so that the dress looks like it is on the hanger when viewed from the front. Use the hook of the hanger to hang up the notepad.

If you don't have any extra paper doll clothes to use for the cover, try finding a pretty dress in a magazine or catalog to use instead. If the paper dress seems too flimsy, glue it to light cardboard.

45

Happy Hanger

Give your closet hangers some personality with this idea!

Here is what you need:

Styrofoam tray to work on

wire clothes hanger

1½-inch (3.75-cm) Styrofoam ball

poster paint in the skin color of your choice and a paintbrush

thin ribbon

map pins

two small wiggle eyes

GLUE white craft glue

embroidery floss in the hair color of your choice

Here is what you do:

1. Paint the Styrofoam ball and let it dry on the Styrofoam tray.

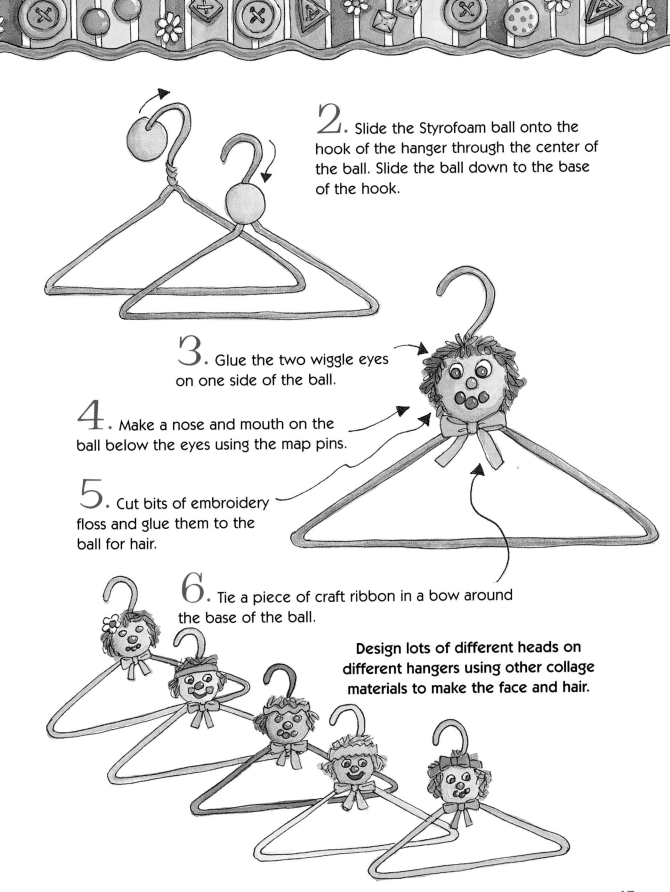

2. Slide the Styrofoam ball onto the hook of the hanger through the center of the ball. Slide the ball down to the base of the hook.

3. Glue the two wiggle eyes on one side of the ball.

4. Make a nose and mouth on the ball below the eyes using the map pins.

5. Cut bits of embroidery floss and glue them to the ball for hair.

6. Tie a piece of craft ribbon in a bow around the base of the ball.

Design lots of different heads on different hangers using other collage materials to make the face and hair.

About the Author

Thirty years as a teacher and director of nursery school programs has given Kathy Ross extensive experience in guiding young children through craft projects. Among the more than forty craft books she has written are *Crafts for All Seasons, The Storytime Craft Book, Kathy Ross Crafts Letter Shapes, All New Crafts for Valentine's Day, All New Crafts for Halloween, All New Crafts for Easter,* and the first book in this series of books for girls, *Things to Make for Your Doll.*

For a complete list of Kathy Ross craft books, visit www.lernerbooks.com, or to find out more about the author, visit www.kathyross.com.